I0820582

Štěpánka Sekaninová
Linh Dao

GROWING UP LADYBUG

albatros

SPRING IS HERE. TIME TO GET UP!

Aa-aah! I simply have to stretch. After sleeping all winter long, I feel soooo stiff! Fortunately, spring is here. Why lie around and dream when you can jump out of bed? Hi, I'm Mariella, and we are all seven-spot ladybugs. I'm so excited for you to get to know us. Come on!

Zzzzzzzz...
Oh!
Is it time to
get up?

ABOUT LADYBUGS

As I was explaining, we ladybugs live all over the world, except perhaps in the polar regions. You probably know why we sleep in winter. After all, what would we do in the snow? We spend a lot of our time alone, but gather together to hibernate under stones, or in crevices. A bunch of us together is called a loveliness—how perfect is that?

WHERE DO WE LIVE?

Ladybugs live in meadows, forests, cities, river valleys, gardens, fields, and by streams and ponds. We're not choosy. But we must always have food nearby.

SEVEN SPOTS OR MORE?

Did you know that there are lots of ladybugs in the world? People in the know put the number of species at 5,000. Not all have seven dots like me, of course. Just look at some of my cousins! Nothing like me, are they? But one thing is for sure—we all look very stylish!

EYED LADYBUG

I think big: I can have more than twenty spots. I live in coniferous trees. It can be hard to see me high up in the pine tree branches.

CREAM-SPOT LADYBUG

What's the big thing about black spots? I much prefer white ones.

MULTICOLORED ASIAN LADYBUG

There's nothing like variety! The more traditional among us have red elytra and black spots. The more daring favor black elytra and red spots. Both looks are great!

TWO-SPOTTED LADYBUG

Less is more, I tell myself.
I choose simplicity. Two
spots are enough for me.
I'm just as useful as a ladybug
with lots of spots.

22-SPOT LADYBUG

Why is red so common when
a bug feels better in yellow?
My favorite food is all
fungus that harms plants.

TEN-SPOTTED LADYBUG

We may be called ten-spotted
ladybugs, but the number of
our spots varies. Some of us
have fifteen, some none at all.
You'll find us most often on
our favorite yellow flowers.

BRAVE HUNTERS

Humans are very fond of ladybugs. When you're out and about, the sight of us always brings a smile to your lips. It is said that we bring you luck. We kill aphids that attack your crops and flowers, so you should be glad when we settle in your gardens or fields.

ON THE HUNT

We may look peaceable at first glance, but actually we are fearless warriors and hunters. Aphids and worms, should be very afraid! They can't escape us! I can catch up to 5,000 aphids in one year. Quite a good score, don't you think?

ENEMY ON THE HORIZON

Strange to say, even beautiful, beloved ladybugs have enemies—predators keen to sink their teeth and greedy beaks into us! But ladybugs never give up without a fight. We have highly effective secret weapons, which we use without mercy when confronted by someone wishing to feast on us.

My elytra are my armor!

DEFENSE NO. 1

Take our hard shells. Many a bug-eating insect will struggle to bite through them.

DEFENSE NO. 2

Our coloring—in my case red elytra with black spots—isn't just for show. Look at that bird with the sharp beak flying away, scared by the sight of me!

DEFENSE NO. 3

Bad smell! Creatures with no smell attract no interest, and we are great at being odorless. But when a hungry predator is approaching, we spray a stinky substance—from our knees—to spoil their appetite.

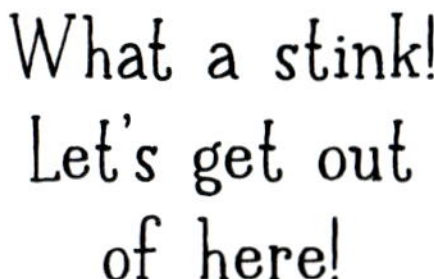

DEFENSE NO. 4

Taste us and you risk a stomachache! As you decide what to do, our body releases a wonderfully bitter, pretty disgusting poisonous substance.

DEFENSE NO. 5

Playing possum: We fall to the ground and lie there apparently helpless, hoping that this will deter the predator. If it doesn't, we release the foul-smelling poison you know about already. Pretty good, right?

LADYBUG COURTSHIP

It's spring, the sun is shining, the flowers are blooming and fragrant, and there are plenty of aphids for me to eat. What more could I wish for? Well, I'd like to have little ladybugs. I'm old enough. I've lived through one whole winter. It's time to find a mate.

Then John asked me to marry him.
The wedding came soon after.

BABIES ON THE WAY

I'm expecting children—lots and lots of them! I have many, many eggs. I found a place where aphids hang out, giving us plenty to eat at all times. Right after that, I laid my eggs.

HEY, EGGS!

I'm delighted with my beautiful yellow eggs. I've placed them upright with great care, packing them together neatly. There's plenty of room for them on these leaves.

THEY MUST EAT!

Some eggs are empty. If the food runs out, my newborns will be able to feed on them.

AN EGG IN CLOSE-UP

To allow air to reach the future ladybugs, all the eggs have a ring of tiny, barely noticeable holes on top.

My little ladybug girls and boys will soon hatch. I can hardly wait! But how will I tell when they are coming?

The eggs have darkened. The little larvae inside are gnawing away, now mature enough to be eager for something new.

HAPPY MOM

I'm a mom! The proud mom of lots of little ladybugs! Aren't they cute? I know they don't look much like me. In fact, you could compare them to dragons from a fairy tale. But believe it or not, I used to look like that, too. I really did!

JOYS AND WORRIES OF HAVING CHILDREN

My babies are growing like crazy. They don't actually need me at all. All they do is eat, eat, walk, and call, "Mom, look at me!" Eating all those aphids helps them develop and grow strong. Soon, they will pupate and become beautiful ladybugs like their parents.

We have no fear of enemies. I know that dangers lurk in the world for my offspring, but their yellow-orange spots are enough to frighten anyone away! When larvae are afraid, they give off a bad smell and taste bitter. That spoils the appetite of even the hungriest predators!

MY APHIDS!

On some plants, there are too few aphids. Larvae tug at and fight over them like fidgety children over a toy.

PUPATION TIME

My larvae are growing fast. In fact, they are now so big and fat, they can barely crawl. This can mean only one thing: my babies are ready to pupate! They curl up comfortably on a leaf and wait. It seems that nothing happens for quite a while. But inside each pupa an important transformation is taking place. Nature is working its magic!

Waiting makes
me hungry.
Waiting can be
dangerous, too.
The wait for my
little bugs...
...is a very
long one....

METAMORPHOSIS

The pupae have changed into beetles—hurray! Celebrate with me! Such a metamorphosis doesn't happen just like that. Imagine pulling yourself out of a tight shell when you are still very small and quite weak. My little ladybugs did it!

On emerging from their coverings—or exuviae—ladybugs don't have a single black spot. If you were to touch their elytra, you would find it to be soft and damp. The new ladybugs climb onto a plant to dry. As they dry, the elytra harden and their first pretty spots appear.

MIRACLE OF NATURE

The miracle of a small, eggbound larval dragon turning into a silent pupa turning into an adult ladybug is known as metamorphosis. The whole process looks something like this:

Being a pupa takes a lot of patience.
3. Pupa – 7-14 days
4. The outcome? A ladybug pretty as a picture!

NEW GENERATION

Before you know it, there are new ladybugs in the big, beautiful world. Soon they will be ridding it of harmful aphids and worms, making people glad. Next year, after they wake up from their hibernation, they will be old enough to mate and give birth to more little ones. That's how it goes with ladybugs.

AUTUMN IS HERE

Autumn has arrived. My young ladybugs are soaking up the last of the sun's rays. To survive the harsh, long winter, they need to gather a sufficient supply of food. Having done both, they find a shelter, where they build a common bedroom. As the year ends, they are fully prepared for their long sleep.

Shine a little more,
sun, to keep us
warm for winter.

z z z

GOOD NIGHT!

Shhhhh! The new ladybugs, whose birth and growth you have witnessed, are getting ready for bed, shaking out blankets and turning off lights. They drop off to sleep one by one. Outside snow is falling. Spring seems far away. The little spotted beetles dream about the meadow, tasty aphids, the forest, fields, gardens in bloom, the big, wide world, and the sun's first warm rays. We will leave them to it. Good night, everyone!

GROWING UP LADYBUG

5. května 1746/22, Prague 4, Czech Republic
Author: Štěpánka Sekaninová
Illustrator: © Linh Dao, 2024
Editor: Susan Marston
Translator: Andrew Oakland
Proofreader: Susan Marston
Graphics and typesetting: Adéla Imreczeová,
Kristýna Krahulcová, Roman Havlice

Printed in China by Leo Paper Products Ltd.

www.albatrosbooks.com

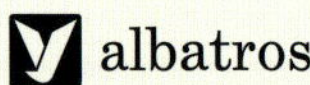